FIRENZE
MVSEI

Accademia Gallery

Franca Falletti
Director of the Accademia Gallery

G GIUNTI

Graphic design: Franco Bulletti
Cover design: Laura Belforte *and* Fabio Filippi
Floor plans: Stefano Benini
Page Format: Edimedia Sas, Florence

Editorial manager: Claudio Pescio
Editing: Augusta Tosone
Translation: Ailsa Wood for Lexis, Florence *and* Catherine Frost

Photographic credits:
Archivio Giunti / Foto Rabatti-Domingie, Florence
Photographs of the David *restored (2004):*
Archivio Giunti / Antonio Quattrone, Florence

www. giunti.it

First edition: October 1998
Updated edition: September 2009

"FIRENZE MVSEI" is a registered trademark
created by Sergio Bianco

Contents

MICHELANGELO BUONARROTI, *David*, detail, after the 2004 restoration

ENOUGH BOOKS HAVE been written about the public museums in Florence run by the Soprintendenza Speciale per il Polo Museale fiorentino to fill a large library. This is hardly surprising when one considers that the artistic heritage preserved in our museums has been famous throughout the world for centuries. For hundreds of years writers, scholars and travellers of every nationality and country have been attempting to describe all that the Florentine museums contain. They have made great efforts to explain why these museums are so fascinating, and to lead a path through paintings and sculptures for both the uninformed but willing visitor and the refined and jaded intellectual.

Over time, however, the museums have altered their aspect and their layout, the exhibitions have been arranged in new ways, the collections have been enriched (or impoverished). Attributions of works in the museums have also changed, restorations have transformed the appearance of many pieces, the rise and fall of aesthetic tendencies have led to reorganisation and the exhibition of differing works. All these things are constantly taking place within the public collections because museology and the history of art, like any intellectual endeavour, are in a constant state of progress and transformation. This explains why the literature surrounding the Florentine museums (like that of any of the world's great art collections) is so immense, and in a process of continual updating and change.

The perfect, definitive guide to a museum, any museum, does not and cannot exist. The premise seems obvious, but is nonetheless necessary in order to understand the point of the publication introduced by these lines. From the moment when, in accordance with the application of the Ronchey law 4/93, the Giunti publishing house group took over the running of the support services within the Florentine museum system, it was decided to start at once on a standardised series of illustrated guides. These guides, displaying the cuneiform flower of 'Firenze Musei' on the cover, guarantee that at the year of publication the state of each museum is exactly that described in the guide.

Certain things are obviously necessary if a museum guide is to aspire to reliability, official standing and at the same time enjoy a wide distribution: accuracy of information, high quality reproductions, an easily manageable format, a reasonable cost and – not least – a clearly written text (without, naturally, being banal or lacking in precision). Readers will judge for themselves if the guide which follows this introduction reaches these standards. I have no doubt that this will be a serious and committed judgement, just as myself and the Publisher of this guide have been serious and committed in attempting to meet the cultural needs of whoever visits our museums in the best way and with every possible care.

Antonio Paolucci

Lorenzo Monaco, *Christ as the Man of Sorrows*

THE ACCADEMIA GALLERY

THE ACCADEMIA GALLERY is one of the best known museums in the world today, and during the eleven hours it is open on an average day, it is visited by up to six thousand tourists, making a total of almost a million visitors per year. The Gallery is situated on the former site of a monastery, San Matteo, and a convent, San Niccolò di Cafaggio, which occupied the whole block between piazza Santissima Annunziata and via Ricasoli. Its collection consists of works of art from the Accademia del Disegno (Academy of Drawing), founded by Cosimo I de' Medici in 1563, and from the Accademia di Belle Arti (Academy of Fine Arts), an art school founded by Grand Duke Pietro Leopoldo of Lorraine in 1784. The aim of this collection of works was thus originally didactic, and useful to young artists who could study and copy the great examples of the past.

The abolition of monasteries and ecclesiastical brotherhoods in 1785 and 1808 brought numerous religious paintings to the rooms of the recently founded school, and many of these are still part of the Gallery's vast collection of paintings today.

Then in 1873, Michelangelo's *David*, previously situated in Piazza della Signoria in front of Palazzo Vecchio, was also transferred to the Accademia, which subsequently began to be known throughout the world as the Michelangelo Museum. In 1909 it was joined by the *Slaves* and *Saint Matthew*, and in 1939, the *Pietà from Palestrina*. In the meantime, the collection of paintings was continually diminishing: Beato Angelico's pictures were transferred to the San Marco Museum where they are still displayed today, and many masterpieces were moved to the Uffizi Gallery.

Since 1980 the Gallery has been considerably enlarged. A collection of plaster casts by the 19th century sculptors Lorenzo Bartolini and Luigi Pampaloni has been set up in the huge room on the ground floor, known as the 'room of the Tuscans'. The highly prized collection of late Gothic Florentine paintings has been situated on the first floor, in four rooms which were not previously used for permanent exhibitions, along with the unique group of Russian icons from the private collections of the Grand Dukes of Lorraine.

Lastly, in May 2001, a section dedicated to musical instruments was inaugurated, through an agreement stipulated with the nearby 'Luigi Cherubini' State Conservatory of Music, owner of the priceless Collection of instruments that once belonged to the Grand Dukes of Tuscany (the Medici and Lorraine families). The Accademia di Belle Arti from which, as has been seen, this museum originated, had a sector dedicated to musical education, of which the Conservatory is today the heir. With this last acquirement the Galleria has thus re-established links with its historical roots.

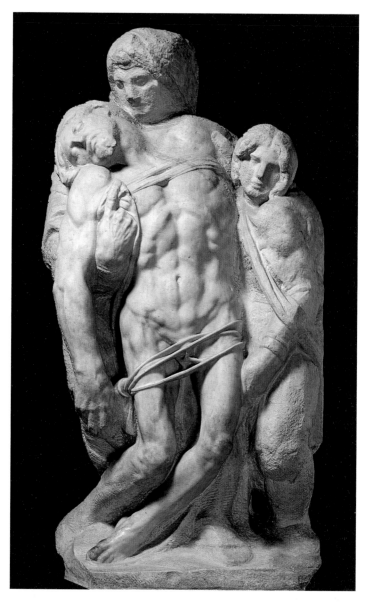

MICHELANGELO BUONARROTI (?), *Pietà from Palestrina*

THE COLLECTION OF GOLD-BACKGROUND PANELS

The Accademia Gallery's unique collection of panels painted on gold background is located on the ground floor, in three rooms adjacent to the left side wing of the Tribuna, and the four rooms on the first floor. Various subsequent additions have enlarged the collection, which was recently rearranged, in accordance with the latest critical studies of the subject, to allow these Florentine works of art from the period between Giotto and Masaccio to be seen clearly and completely. The three ground floor rooms house the works of late 13th century painters, the contemporaries of Giotto, Taddeo Gaddi and Bernardo Daddi, and the Orcagna family, leading figures in Florence after the great plague of 1348. On the first floor are works by both lesser artists and great masters, which exemplify the various trends of late Gothic painting in the Tuscan capital. The greatest of these are the intense *Christ in Pietà* painted by Giovanni da Milano and the shining panels by Lorenzo Monaco, each phase of whose work is recorded here. All the works are from religious buildings in Florence and the rest of Tuscany and some polyptychs are still complete with cusps, pinnacles, newels and spiral side posts, and predellas, providing us with an opportunity to understand the complexity and perfection such items required from carpenters and carvers.

FIFTEENTH AND SIXTEENTH CENTURY PAINTINGS

The collection of paintings from the 15th and 16th centuries, which is displayed in the so-called Hall of the Colossus, in the *Slaves* Gallery and in the Tribuna of the *David*, contains works representative of the leading figures and the major trends in art in Florence during this time of crucial cultural importance to the city. From the fifteenth century are exhibited works by masters influenced by Fra Angelico and Masaccio, such as Andrea di Giusto Manzini and Paolo Uccello; from the second half of the century are Domenico del Ghirlandaio, Botticelli and Filippino Lippi, to mention only the most famous. Dating from the early 16th century is the majestic *Vallombrosa Altarpiece* by Perugino as well as several fine works by Granacci, Ridolfo del Ghirlandaio and Sogliani. In the Gallery of the *Slaves* are works by Andrea del Sarto, Fra Bartolomeo and other great masters from the same period. In the two side wings of the Tribune hang paintings by Michelangelo's contemporaries, providing a splendid setting for the gigantic statue of *David*, even more striking today after its recent restoration and the new arrangement of the hall. On the right, in the shorter wing, works by artists from the most representative current of Mannerism, such as Portelli, Poppi and Salviati, are displayed; on the left, instead, are four great altarpieces by the painters of the Counter-Reformation: Bronzino, his pupil Alessandro Allori, Santi di Tito and his pupil Cosimo Gamberucci.

MICHELANGELO'S SCULPTURES

The *David* was the first of Michelangelo's sculptures to be displayed in the Accademia Gallery. It was brought here in 1873, allegedly for conservation reasons; but although quite serious damage was undoubtedly caused by the long centuries passed under the elements and bad restoration works, many other factors were involved in the decision to remove the masterpiece from its original location in Piazza della Signoria. The intention was actually to hold a large exhibition dedicated to Michelangelo to celebrate the fourth centenary of his birth, in 1875, and subsequently set up a real Michelangelo Museum with original works, plaster casts and drawings. This duly took place: around the period of the First World War the museum displayed, alongside the works we can still admire today, the *Fiume Torso*, now in Casa Buonarroti and the *Victory* group, now in the Palazzo Vecchio. There were also numerous plaster casts of the great artist's works, which were preserved in other Italian and foreign collections. Lastly, in 1939, the *Pietà* discovered in the Barberini Chapel in Palestrina, near Rome, was brought here; Michelangelo's authorship of this work is however denied today by the most authoritative experts.

THE NINETEENTH CENTURY ROOM

In 1985, works by teachers from the 19th century Accademia were displayed in the pleasant space which used to be the passageway for women from the San Matteo Hospital. The collection of plaster casts, in particular, has found its permanent home here, which was donated to the Italian State by the heirs of the sculptor Lorenzo Bartolini after his death in 1850.

Alongside these are casts by another great 19th century Tuscan sculptor, Luigi Pampaloni, and some paintings closely linked to the history of the Accademia; these were painted by pupils who later became famous artists (like Silvestro Lega or Cesare Mussini) when they were admitted to the Accademia or when they completed their studies. The plaster casts displayed are nearly all models made by the artist and not, as one might think, casts of finished works. They should therefore be considered more autographical than the final marble versions, as they were made by the artist in person. Bartolini in particular had a highly organised studio, which often continued his work while he was away. In order for the finished work to be the same as the model, dark dots had to be followed, which can still be seen on many casts and are actually iron nails inserted while the plaster was still wet. The large number of busts here are proof of the popularity of the portraiture genre with the 19th century European bourgeoisie, prior to the advent of photography.

THE MUSEUM OF MUSICAL INSTRUMENTS

by Gabriele Rossi Rognoni

MUSIC AT THE MEDICEAN COURT

The Museum of Musical Instruments in the Accademia Gallery, inaugurated in 2001, currently exhibits over forty instruments from the 17th, 18th and 19th centuries, coming from the Grand-Ducal collections of the Medici and Lorraine families. The collection is owned by the 'Luigi Cherubini' Conservatory of Florence, which has carefully preserved the instruments since the 19th century. The exhibition includes objects unique the world over, such as the Tenor Viola *by Antonio Stradivari, the only instrument created by him which has remained entirely in its original state; the earliest known example of an* Upright Piano; *and an* Oval Spinet, *the first instrument constructed for the Medici family by the inventor of the piano, Bartolomeo Cristofori. The cultural context for which these instruments were created is illustrated by some 17th century paintings portraying musicians at the Medicean Court. A computerized multimedia system provides visitors with information in Italian and English on the history and particular features of these instruments, and even allows them to hear their sounds. Some models which can be actuated by visitors illustrate the action of the first* Piano, *invented at the Medicean Court in the late 17th century, and show how this instrument differs from its forerunner, the* Harpsichord. *A room dedicated to Alessandro Kraus, a Florentine collector from the late 19th century who owned over a thousand instruments coming from all over the world, has recently been added to the Museum. Some of these instruments recently donated to the Museum by a descendent of the collector, Mirella Gatti-Kraus, are displayed here.*

ANTON DOMENICO GABBIANI
The Grand Prince Ferdinando with his Musicians
(whole and detail on facing page)

1685 (?)
Oil on canvas
139×221
(From the Palatine Gallery Storage, Florence)
Inv. 1890 no. 2808

Music played a primary role in the official celebrations of the Medicean Court, as another manifestation of the dynasty's power. It was at the Court of Ferdinando I de' Medici that, in 1500, a theatrical performance which was entirely sung, *Euridice* by Iacopo Peri, was represented for the first time, and the chronicles of the time describe grandiose musical events held in the churches and public squares, as well as splendid concerts given for the nobility and foreign emissaries.

A vivacious musical current independent of State occasions was promoted in particular by the son of Cosimo III, Grand Prince Ferdinando, himself a musician and lover of music who attracted to Florence such leading composers of the day as Georg Friedrich Haendel and Alessandro Scarlatti. His interest in music also led him to build up an extraordinary collection of over one hundred musical instruments, some of which come from the hands of the most famous makers of the epoch. The instruments displayed in the first section of the Museum come from the collection of Grand Prince Ferdinando.

The musicians and their instruments at the Court of Ferdinando were portrayed by Anton Domenico Gabbiani in a cycle of canvases painted between 1685 and 1690. These representations are so faithful that it has been possible in some cases to identify the personages and to recognize the instruments from the descriptions in the Medicean Inventories.

THE MEDICEAN VIOLONCELLOS

The three *Cellos* are listed in an Inventory of the instruments belonging to the personal collection of Grand Prince Ferdinando de' Medici, compiled in the year 1700. The one bearing the Medici coat-of-arms was built by the violinmaker from Cremona Nicolò Amati, active between 1630 and 1670, and probably the master of Antonio Stradivari. The body of the instrument, originally larger, was 'trimmed' in the late 18th century to reduce its size to the dimensions that had become standard for Cellos after the beginning of 1700.

NICOLÒ AMATI
Violoncello

c. 1650

Red spruce
and maple wood
Total length 122 cm
Body measurements:
length 75.7 cm;
maximum width 45.7 cm
Inv. Cherubini 1988/33

MARBLE DULCIMER

The *Dulcimer* is an instrument that was extraordinarily popular in Italy in the 17th and 18th centuries, only to disappear completely in the Romantic age. With the ingenious arrangement of the strings, which were plucked with plectra fastened to the fingertips, a wide range of notes can be played with this small instrument.

The one exhibited here is truly unique in that it is entirely constructed of marble of three different kinds (white statuary marble, bardiglio from Carrara and yellow broccatello) rather than wood.

The dedication and the painting on the cover

of the case show that it was built for Grand Duke Cosimo III de' Medici, the father of Grand Prince Ferdinando, after 1691.

It was probably the work of the same artisan who built for the Este family (for whom he work-

ed from 1686 to 1687) a *Guitar*, a *Violin*, a *Harpsichord* and various wind instruments, all in the same material.

Although these instruments were designed primarily as decorative objects, they could perfectly well be played.

MICHELE ANTONIO GRANDI
Marble Dulcimer
(whole and detail above)

After 1691

Statuary marble, bardiglio, and yellow broccatello
Maximum width 74.5 cm;
depth 30 cm
Inv. Cherubini 1988/88

THE MEDICEAN QUINTET

The *Tenor Viola* and the *Violoncello* formed part of a 'quintet' of string instruments (two *Violins*, an *Alto Viola*, a *Tenor Viola* and a *Violoncello*) built by the master from Cremona Antonio Stradivari for Grand Prince Ferdinando and dated 1690. The five instruments were all decorated with the Medici coat-of-arms in mother-of-pearl, and with ebony and ivory inlays. The chosen woods, of exceptional quality, combined excellent sound with the highest aesthetic value.

The *Tenor Viola* is the only instrument in the world made by Antonio Stradivari to be entirely conserved in its original state; as such, it represents a document of inestimable importance for violin-makers and music scholars.

The large size of the *Viola* body, like that of the *Violoncello*, intensifies the bass sounds and confers on the instruments a characteristic deep timbre.

ANTONIO STRADIVARI
"Medici" Tenor Viola
(whole and details)

1690

Red spruce
and maple wood
Total length 75.5 cm
Body measurements:
length 47.8 cm;
maximum width 27.1 cm
Inv. Cherubini 1988/15

VIOLINS

The three *Violins* were acquired for the Grand-Ducal Collection at a relatively late time (after 1814), but were constructed during the lifetime of Grand Prince Ferdinando. The red-varnished *Violin* is one of the best conserved instruments built by Antonio Stradivari. It dates from the period of full stylistic maturity of the Master, who established the classic proportions and lines for the violin makers in Cremona, still today taken as model by violin-makers all over the world. The other two instruments, of the Modena and the Po Valley schools, differ from each other in the color of the varnish, the contour of the belly, the shape of the f-holes and the form of the scroll. On the basis of this and other stylistic features, their authorship (falsely indicated on labels glued to the inside of the body) has been questioned and the current attribution has been proposed.

ANTONIO STRADIVARI
"Medici" Violin

1716
Red spruce
and maple wood
Total length 59.7 cm
Body measurements:
length 35.8 cm;
maximum width 20.8 cm
Inv. Cherubini 1988/3

KEYBOARD
INSTRUMENTS

The *Piano*, a keyboard
instrument whose strings
are struck by hammers,
was invented in Floren-
ce shortly before 1700
by a Paduan instrument-
maker, Bartolomeo Cri-
stofori, at the service of
Grand Prince Ferdinan-
do, and was only the most
long-lasting of his nu-
merous and ingenious
inventions. Exhibited in
the same room is the first
instrument created by
him for the Medici: a
Spinet recently redis-
covered, whose form,
action and sonority were
entirely designed by Bar-
tolomeo Cristofori. Dat-
ing from slightly later,
also built for the Medici,
is a *Harpsichord* con-
structed entirely of ebo-
ny wood. The action dis-
played at the left of the
Spinet seems instead to
come from a pianoforte
dating from Cristofori's
time, although its attri-
bution to a specific mak-
er is still debatable. The
instrument displayed on
the opposite side of the
hall is the earliest known
Upright Piano. It was
built in 1739, seven years
after the death of Cri-
stofori, by an instrument-
maker who may have
been his assistant, Do-
menico del Mela.

DOMENICO DEL MELA
Upright Piano
1739
Coniferous wood,
cypress and boxwood

Total height 273 cm;
width 93 cm;
depth 64 cm
Compass:
Do1/Mi1-Do5 (C/E-c''')
Inv. Cherubini 1988/110

18

MUSIC IN THE LORRAINE AGE

When the sovereignty of the Grand-Duchy of Tuscany passed from the Medici family (which died out in 1737) to the Austrian one of the Lorraines, radical changes occurred in the musical life of the Court and that of the entire city. Grand Duke Pietro Leopoldo (ruler of Florence from 1765) promoted public musical events, held in the streets and squares, as well as celebrations open on occasion to the citizens as a whole. This new approach was reflected in the collection of musical instruments as well. Many of the instruments from Medicean times, worn and unsuited to the new activity of the Court, were sold or discarded, and new ones – wind and percussion instruments in particular – were purchased and imported from abroad.

PERCUSSION INSTRUMENTS

The percussion instruments exhibited here represent one of the very rare homogenous groups of this kind which has survived from the late 18th century. These instruments were used for the most part in theatrical performances and Court balls.

Among them is the oldest pair of *Kettle-drums* in Italy, equipped with a tuning mechanism, in addition to pairs of *Jingles* used "for the waltz of the whip", *Xylophones*, *Castanets* and *Triangles*.

JOHANN CASPAR JOSEPH EINBIGLER (?)
Pair of kettle-drums

c. 1837

Copper, iron, leather
Height of the drumhead
from the ground 80 cm;
diameter of the drumheads:
50/53 cm
Inv. Cherubini 1988/199, 209

WIND INSTRUMENTS

After the Restoration of the Lorraines in 1814, subsequent to fifteen years of French domination, various wind instruments were purchased for both theatrical use and performances of the Grand-Ducal band. The brass instruments, *Horns* and *Trombones*, were imported from Germany and Austria and may have been brought to Florence by members of the Court. The provenance of the little *Post-horn* (before 1819) is instead unknown, but the instrument is of a type that had been commonly used since the early 16th century by couriers in the postal service to announce their arrival at a post station. In the nineteenth century the little instrument was used to limited extent for special effects in the orchestra.

The next display case holds wind instruments made of wood. Some of them, a *Piccolo* (before 1806), a *Basset-Horn* (1810-1819) and the five *Clarinets* (from about 1838) are furnished with *corps de rechange* which could be substituted to the original ones to change the intonation and make it more acute.

Some others, such as the *Serpent* and the above-mentioned *Basset-Horn*, are constructed so that the size of these quite long instruments can be reduced, making them more manageable. The *Serpent* was widely used as bass accompaniment for religious and military music, while passages for the *Basset-Horn* were composed by W. A. Mozart, among others.

LORENZO CERINO
Serpent

Late 18th century
Chestnut wood (?)
and leather
Overall length 86 cm;
length of tube
about 195 cm
Inv. Cherubini 1988/175

THE TRUMPET MARINE

The sound of this instrument with a single catgut string is extraordinarily similar to that of a trumpet, thanks to an asymmetrical bridge that rests on only one of its two feet, while the other rattles on the soundboard when the string is bowed.

This instrument, which entered the Grand-Ducal Collection in the late 18th century, was used in musical performances held at the Lorraine Court until the 1830s. It was specifically required in the score of an opera presented at Court, the *Socrate immaginario* by Giovanni Paisiello, in which an instrumental solo is followed by an aria ("Questa corda non s'accorda al dio Amor" [this string is not in tune with the god of Love]), a humorous allusion to the instrument's harsh timbre.

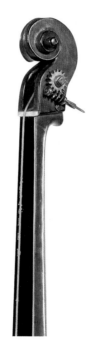

ANONYMOUS
Trumpet Marine
(whole and detail)

Late 18th century

White spruce, cherry and walnut wood
Total height 162.4 cm; maximum width 29.2 cm
Inv. Cherubini 1988/47

21

HURDY-GURDIES

The sound of the *Hurdy-gurdy* is produced by a number of strings set in vibration by a wooden wheel coated with rosin, driven by a crank, which strokes the strings like the bow of a violin. The notes are produced by pressing a series of keys on the side with the left hand. Instruments based on this principle had been known in Europe since the 13th century, but only in the 18th this model, richly decorated with mother-of-pearl and inlays, was developed specifically for amateur musicians among the nobility. The *Hurdy-gurdy* became especially popular in France, since the wife of Louis XV was in fact an accomplished player on this instrument. In a parallel development, a 'popular' model, much cruder in appearance but functioning in the same way and used mainly by beggars, survived throughout the 19th century.

JEAN NICOLAS LAMBERT
Pair of Hurdy-gurdies

1775
Mahogany, maple, beech, ebony, ivory
Body measurements:
length 46.1 cm;
maximum width 24.5 cm
Inv. Cherubini 1988/50-51

THE VIOLA
AND THE GUITARS

The *Viola*, the *Piano-Guitar* and the *Guitar with six strings* entered the Lorraine Collection in the early 19th century, and were probably purchased during the period of French domination. The *Viola* (1774), which still has its original neck, presents the typical characteristics of a German-made instrument: dark varnish, short, vertical f-holes, pronounced arching of the belly and back.

The *Piano-Guitar* is, instead, an instrument constructed in the United States near the end of the 18th century, but designed in Great Britain as a particular version of the *English Guitar*, with drop-shape case, flat belly and back. It was an instrument de-signed for well-brought up young girls, in which the strings are struck by a series of hammers actioned by six keys, ensuring that the player's fingertips are not rough-ened. The *Guitar with six strings*, despite some modifications made to the original structure, has kept the slender proportions of the body typical of instruments built in the first half of the 19th century.

This instrument was played, it seems, by Queen Maria Luisa di Borbone-Parma (1807).

ANONYMOUS
Guitar with six strings

ante 1804
Spruce and exotic wood
Total length 91.5 cm
Body measurements:
length 43.2 cm
maximum width 26.1 cm
Inv. Cherubini 1988/73

HALL OF THE COLOSSUS

The name of this room is not, as is usually believed, taken from Giambologna's plaster model, now placed at its center, but from the model of one of the Dioscuri *of Montecavallo, displayed here in the 19th century. The panels exhibited here belong 15th and early 16th century Forentine painting. They include master-pieces such as the canvas depicting* Scenes of Monastic Life *by Paolo Uccello and the* Madonna and Child with the Young Saint John and Two Angels *by Botticelli. The production of the most important workshops of Renaissance Florence, such as those of Ghirlandaio, Cosimo Rosselli, Perugino and Filippino Lippi, is also represented.*

GIAMBOLOGNA
*Rape of the
Sabine Women*

1582

Plaster cast
Height 410
Sculptures Inv. no. 1071

This is the plaster model for the marble sculptured group which can be seen under the Loggia dei Lanzi in Piazza della Signoria.
Giambologna's virtuosity here ventures to create for the first time a large-sized marble sculpture with a tightly-knit group of three figures, which almost form a single body, in a circular spiral movement seemingly without beginning or end. When the group was sculpted it did not have a definite subject but was presented by the artist as a simple exercise in skill; only later was it given the title *Rape of the Sabine Women*.

24

PAOLO UCCELLO
*Scenes
of Hermit Life*
(whole and detail)

c. 1460

Oil on canvas; 81×111
Inv. 1890 no. 5381

The subject of this painting by Paolo Uccello is not easily interpreted but is certainly linked to a path of meditation and spiritual improvement through prayer. The following episodes can be identified: *The Stigmata of Saint Francis, Saint Jerome worships the Crucifix, The Appearance of the Virgin to Saint Bernard* and *Saint Benedict preaches to His Brethren.*

LO SCHEGGIA
Cassone Adimari
(whole and details)

c. 1450

Tempera on wood
63×280
Inv. 1890 no. 8457

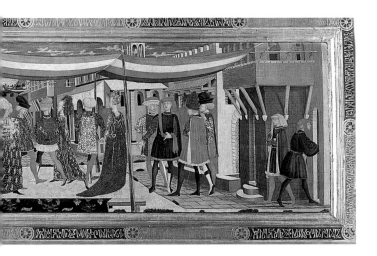

This was originally listed as *Cassone Adimari* because it was thought to be the front panel of a wedding chest belonging to the Adimari family. The painting was later recognised as part of a *spalliera*, a wall decoration, and was attributed to Giovanni di Ser Giovanni, known as Lo Scheggia, the brother of Masaccio. The images depicted here concern a wedding feast and portray the streets, monuments (the Baptistry can be seen on the left), landscapes and customs of Renaissance Florence with vivacity and extraordinary wealth of detail.

SANDRO BOTTICELLI
*Madonna and Child
with the Young Saint
John and Two Angels*
c. 1468
Tempera on wood; 85×64
Inv. 1890 no. 3166

This work is from Botticelli's early phase; the pleasant composition clearly shows the stylistic characteristics of Filippo Lippi, in whose studio Sandro was still training. This composition was to be very successful in later years, repeated in numerous plaster or terra-cotta bas-reliefs for private devotional use.

SANDRO BOTTICELLI (?)
Madonna of the Sea

c. 1475-1480

Tempera on wood
40×28
Inv. 1890 no. 8456

This small panel, which owes its name to the lovely distant seascape in the background, has always been one of the most admired works by visitors to the Gallery.

Its attribution, however, is still debated by art historians, some believing it to be the work of Sandro Botticelli, others that of the young Filippino Lippi.

COSIMO ROSSELLI
Saint Barbara

c. 1470
Tempera on wood
215×219
Inv. 1890 no. 8635

Cosimo Rosselli, head of a well-equipped, active family-run studio, painted this gorgeous panel for the chapel of Saint Barbara and Saint Quiricus in the basilica of the Santissima Annunziata in Florence. This chapel belonged to the so-called 'Teutonic nation', i.e. to the Germans and Flemings. Saint Barbara was the patron saint of artillery and therefore she is holding up the tower as a symbol of a line of fortification and crushing a conquered warrior beneath her feet. The composition of the painting recalls details from works by other contemporary Florentine artists, like Pollaiuolo's panel for the Portuguese cardinal's chapel in San Miniato and Ghirlandaio's fresco in the church of Sant'Andrea in Cercina, but it is painted with skill and dignity.

ANDREA DI GIUSTO MANZINI
Madonna of the Girdle

1437
Tempera on wood
185×220
Inv. 1890 no. 3236

This painting, which is signed "Andrea de Florentia", comes from the church of Santa Margherita a Cortona (Arezzo), and is the work of a Florentine painter active during the first half of the 15th century. The artist is clearly familiar with the examples of his peers, other painters such as Paolo Uccello and Fra Angelico, but solidly linked to the Gothic tradition, as this altarpiece shows in its use of gold-leaf background and the division of the space into three, which recalls the 14th century polyptychs.

GIOVANNI ANTONIO
SOGLIANI
Dispute over
the Immaculate
Conception

c. 1530

Oil on canvas
347×230
Inv. 1890 no. 3203

This panel shows the Doctors of the Church gathered around the body of Adam discussing the question of the Immaculate Conception of the Virgin Mary, a theme also depicted in Carlo Portelli's panel on the left side of the Tribuna beside the *David*. This work belongs to the specific historical period in which the Catholic Church was particularly intent on consolidating the Marian cult against diffusion of the Lutheran heresy.

LORENZO DI CREDI
Adoration
of the Child

c. 1496-1500
Tempera on wood
156×148.5
Inv. 1890 no. 8661
Restored: 1988

The original location of this painting by Lorenzo di Credi is uncertain, some experts believing it to come from the Convento dell'Annunziata, others from the Convento delle Murate.

Inspired in its overall composition by the better known *Adoration* in the Uffizi Gallery (c. 1480-1485), it dates to the last decade in the Fifteenth century, a period in which Early Renaissance style was undergoing dissolution. Lorenzo di Credi assimilated Leonardo's innovations (both were pupils of Verrocchio) up to the point where they represented a break with the past. In

this painting the symmetrical scheme, the view scaled plane by plane, and the sentimental effects of the figures testify to Lorenzo's rejection of Leonardo's perspective studies as well as his links to Fifteenth century tradition. In the landscape in the background and the small figures of shepherds at the left, the quality of the painting is reminiscent of Piero di Cosimo.

FRA BARTOLOMEO
The Prophet Isaiah
c. 1514-1515
Oil on wood; 169×108
Inv. 1890 nos. 1448 and 1449

These two, recently restored panels, came from the Billi Chapel in the basilica of the Santissima Annunziata in Florence. At their centre was the *Salvator Mundi and the Four Evangelists*, today on show in the Palatina Gallery. Cardinal Carlo de' Medici purchased the three panels in 1631 and placed them in the Medici house in Piazza San Marco. In 1697 Prince Ferdinand took the central altarpiece to Palazzo Pitti as part of his personal collection, while the two *Prophets* were passed on to the Uffizi and then to the Accademia. The two *Prophets* were painted by Fra Bartolomeo immediately after his journey to Rome and are evidence of his meditations on Michelangelo's Sistine Chapel.

**FILIPPINO LIPPI
AND PIETRO PERUGINO**
Deposition
(whole and detail below)

1504 and 1507
Oil on wood
334×225
Inv. 1890 no. 8370

This interesting painting was part of a grand wooden group commissioned by the friars of the Santissima Annunziata of Florence for their high altar. Filippino Lippi began work on it in 1504 and finished all of the upper part except for the body of Christ. He died that same year, and the work was completed in 1507 by Pietro Perugino who also painted the other panels to be inserted in the altar.

DOMENICO GHIRLANDAIO
Saint Stephen between Saints James and Peter

1493
Oil on wood
175×174
Inv. 1890 no. 16221

In the past this panel was attributed to Sebastiano Mainardi, a pupil of Ghirlandaio, but it was recently recognised as work of the master himself.

A few years after it was painted, perhaps in 1513, the figure of Saint Stephen was repainted to look like Saint Jerome, by the hand of Fra Bartolomeo, according to traditional accounts. 19th century restoration work then cancelled this modification. In this composition the touch of Ghirlandaio, noted for his lively narrative and decorative elements, is conspicuous in the unusual majesty of the three sculptural figures which strikingly emerge from the chiaroscuro effect of the niches.

PIETRO PERUGINO
*Assumption
of the Virgin*
1500
Oil on wood
415×246
Inv. 1890 no. 8366

This altarpiece was located on the high altar of the church in the Benedictine monastery of Vallombrosa.

Pietro Perugino painted it with a solid, expert technique using structures and drawings already tested on other, similar great compositions, and dwelling in his usual pleasant way on the decorative details like the Archangel Michael's sophisticated armour on the extreme right.

The Gallery of the Slaves

This large room is shaped like a Latin cross-shaped church at the centre of which, underneath the circular skylight, stands the David. *The side wings and Gallery of the* Slaves *occupy the space of the medieval San Matteo Hospital, while the Tribuna was especially built to the design of the architect Emilio De Fabris between 1873 and 1882. This new construction was the subject of many heated disputes, partly because it seemed too narrow for Michelangelo's majestic statue and the background too fragmented by the relief mouldings. Despite these reservations, which to an extent we share today, the room is particularly charming and is one of the most intensely exciting museum areas in the whole world.*

Standing at the end of the Gallery of the Slaves *and looking towards the* David *it is easy to understand why almost a million tourists visit these rooms every year and why many of them experience a perception of beauty which is strong and sudden enough to almost overwhelm the senses.*

MICHELANGELO
BUONARROTI
Slaves

c. 1530

Marble
Height 267, 277, 256, 263
Sculptures Inv. nos. 1078,
1079, 1080, 1081

The four sculptures were intended to decorate the base of a complicated mausoleum to be raised under the dome of San Pietro in the Vatican, for the remains of Pope Julius II della Rovere. The design had a rather tormented history and after undergoing radical modifications to reduce the size, the mausoleum was placed in San Pietro in Vincoli where it remains to this day. The unfinished *Slaves* were donated after Michelangelo's death to Cosimo I de' Medici and placed by him in the Buontalenti Grotto in Boboli whence they were transferred to the Accademia in 1909. The *Slaves* are a useful introduction to an understanding of Michelangelo's unfinished work: their imperfect forms manage to convey a universal meaning to the sensation of an inhuman struggle to free themselves from the marble, which is evident to everyone who sees them.

MICHELANGELO
BUONARROTI

The Young Slave

(detail on following page)
c. 1530

Marble; Height 256
Sculptures Inv. no. 1080

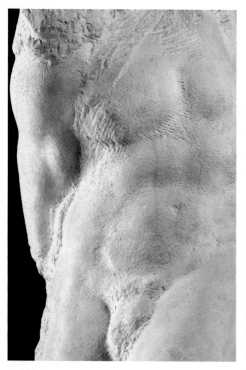

on the right:

MICHELANGELO BUONARROTI

Slaves:
The Awakening Slave

c. 1530

Marble
Height 267
Sculptures Inv. no. 1078

The powerful limbs of this virile figure struggle to emerge from one side of the imposing block of marble.

The roughly outlined features of the face can barely be made out, and the right leg, bent over the left, protrudes forward to mirror the movement of the right arm.

The result is a tense and dynamic composition which fully expresses the struggle of the material to break out of its own limits. In this *Slave* Michelangelo's method of working the marble can be clearly seen, from the stage of roughing out the figure with a chisel to finishing it with the finest blade of the gradine.

The first of the four *Slaves* displayed along the walls of the Gallery leading to the Tribuna of *David* is known as *The Young Slave*. He is depicted with slightly bent knees, as if burdened by a weary step, and his left arm is folded across his face, while his right arm slips behind his hip. Emerging from a block of marble which, at the back, seems still untouched, the different parts of the figure itself have been finished to various degrees: the head is roughly outlined, the left side of the torso more finished than the right. However on each part of the surface the marks of the tools used by Michelangelo in his long creative process are still visible.

Mariotto Albertinelli
Annunciation

1510
Oil on wood
335×230
Inv. 1890 no. 8643

This large panel decorated the chapel of the Brotherhood of San Zanobi at the rectory of the Cathedral of Santa Maria del Fiore in Florence.

After Albertinelli's death two other paintings were added to the sides depicting the *Removal of the body of San Zanobi* and *San Zanobi revives a boy* by Ridolfo del Ghirlandaio, with a stylistic majesty and essentiality perhaps never previously attained in his paintings.

**RIDOLFO
DEL GHIRLANDAIO**
*Removal of the body
of St. Zanobius*
c. 1516
Oil on wood; 219×193
Inv. 1890 no. 1584

This panel, along with the other depicting *St. Zanobius Reviving a Dead Child*, was commissioned by the Compagnia di San Zanobi, to complete the decoration of the altar in the Rectory of Santa Maria del Fiore, over which Mariotto Albertinelli's *Annunciation* had already been placed in 1510. Since these two paintings were smaller it is probable that they were hung on the side walls of the area housing the altar and probably inserted in architectural frames. The pathetic expressions of the faces, individual and naturalistic, the clear, limpid forms and the essential lines of the composition are distinctive features of Ridolfo's style, which finds its maximum expression here.

ANDREA DEL SARTO
Christ as the Man of Sorrows

c. 1525
Detached fresco
182×113
Inv. 1890 no. 8675

This fresco was removed in 1810 from the top of the staircase leading to the novitiate in the Santissima Annunziata monastery in Florence. Despite the poor condition of the work (perhaps also due to the detachment procedure which presented greater risks in that period than today) the figure of the suffering Christ, his pierced hands resting wearily on the stone of the tomb, still expresses the drama of death and pain with great intensity.

**MICHELANGELO
BUONARROTI**
Saint Matthew

1505-1506

Marble
Height 271
Sculptures Inv. no. 1077

The *Saint Matthew* was
originally to be part of
a series of the twelve
apostles, a commission
given to Michelangelo
in 1503 for the columns
of Florence Cathedral.
In the event the sculp-
tor only worked on one,
which is also unfinished,
for which reason it was
left abandoned in the
Opera del Duomo court-
yard, until 1831.
It was moved to the Ac-
cademia di Belle Arti
where it was first placed
in a niche in the court-
yard and later, in 1909,
in the Accademia Galle-
ry near the *Slaves*.

MICHELANGELO
BUONARROTI
Slaves:
The Bearded Slave
(on the left)

c. 1530

Marble
Height 263
Sculptures Inv. no. 1081

The Bearded Slave is the most nearly finished of the four *Slaves*. The face is covered by a thick, curly beard and the thighs are encircled by a strip of cloth. The fine modelling of the torso, the surface finished with soft sensitivity to light and clear evidence of relief modelling, reveals a careful and profound study of anatomy.

Slaves: Atlas
(on the right)

c. 1530

Marble
Height 277
Sculptures Inv. no. 1079

This *Slave* is known as *Atlas* because he seems to be carrying a huge weight on his head; however the weight is in fact the head itself, which is not separate and cannot be distinguished. The legs seem to be parted and the bent arms struggle to support the massive weight bearing down on the wide shoulders.

Pontormo
Venus and Cupid
(whole and details)

c. 1533

Oil on wood
128×194
Inv. 1890 no. 1570

This work was painted by artist Jacopo Carucci, known as Pontormo, on a preparatory cartoon drawn by Michelangelo in 1532-1533, as shown by the sculptural forms of the monumental, statuary Venus counterpoised to the sly Cupid.

Presumably, soon after having been painted, the nude body of Venus was covered with drapery extending from mid-thigh to above the breast, since this is how she appears already in the copy made by Ridolfo del Ghirlandaio, today in Palazzo Colonna in Rome. In 1852 the restorer Ulisse Forni returned the painting to its original aspect by remov-

ing the drapery covering the body of Venus, but added a wisp of fabric over the pubic region.

This too was removed in the recent restoration (2002) which has brought to light and entirely unveiled the original grandiose nude painted by Pontormo.

THE TRIBUNA OF DAVID

**MICHELANGELO
BUONARROTI**
David

1501-1504

Marble
Height 517
Sculptures Inv. no. 1076

The *David* was original-ly commissioned by the Opera del Duomo of Flo-rence to be placed as a decoration in the Cathe-dral. It was sculpted by Michelangelo between 1501 and 1504, when it was placed in front of the Palazzo Vecchio, follow-ing much discussion and debate among the main contemporary Floren-tine artists.

The Giant, as it became known, became a symbol of the civil freedom and virtue of republican Florence, and it remained in its original location until 1873 when it was transferred, using a complex support structure resting on wheels, inside the Accademia di Belle Arti, where it can still be admired today.

The sculpture portrays the future King of Israel in a similar form and pose to a triumphant hero of classical Greece. This clearly distances Michelangelo's *David* from those previously made by Donatello and Verrocchio which, adhering more closely to the biblical text, depicted David as a slender boy, unaware of his divine mission.

The statue's perfect modelling, the calm and determined strength of the expression and its imposing size have made it one of the best-known and most admired works of art in the world.

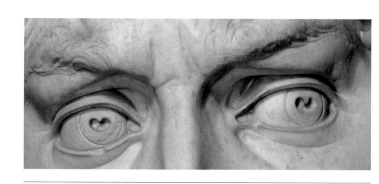

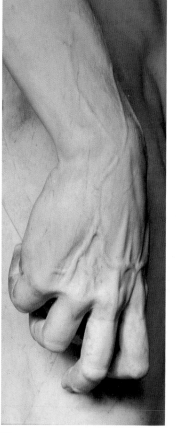

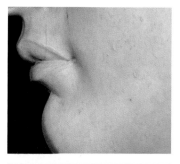

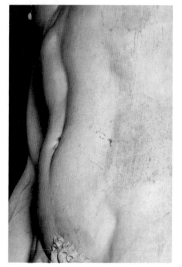

Side wings of the Tribuna

In the early 1980s a number of works by artists who were contemporaries of Michelangelo, or representatives of a slightly younger generation, were placed here. Among these are some of Alessandro Allori's enormous panels.

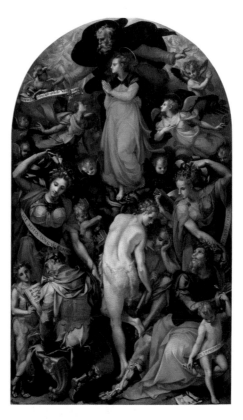

Carlo Portelli
The Immaculate Conception

1566
Oil on wood; 415×246.2
Inv. 1890 no. 4650

The painting, whose recent restoration (2003) has revived its brilliant colors and clear legibil-ity, revealing the splen-did nude Eve, was com-missioned for the church of Ognissanti in Florence. Its subject is the Immac-ulate Conception of Mary, a theme that developed starting from the second half of the 15th century, but was long subjected to heated debate within the Catholic Church. Portelli's strongly Man-nerist style is exempli-fied here in the space en-tirely concentrated in the foreground, and in the poses of his sinuous fig-ures, in studied contrast to one another (those of the Virgin Mary and Eve in particular).

Santi di Tito
*Lamentation
for Christ with the
Virgin, Saint John
the Baptist, Saint
Catherine of Alexandria
and the donor*

c. 1592

Oil on wood
198.5×163,5
Inv. 1890 no. 4637

This painting, which comes from the chapel in Fortezza da Basso (Florence), portrays Christ taken down from the cross, surrounded by the Virgin, St John the Baptist, St Catherine and the donor wearing ornate armor with the insignia of the Knights of Saint Stephen, recently identified as Ernando Sastri of Spain, despite the varying hypotheses suggested by art historians. The particular sensitivity to color, clearly revealed by the restoration (2003), seems to indicate a dating around the 1590s, a period in which Titi was strongly influenced by the colorism of Cigoli.

AGNOLO BRONZINO
Deposition

1560-1561
Oil on wood
349×254
Inv. 1890 no. 3491

Bronzino's enormous painting on wood was commissioned by Cosimo I de' Medici for the church of the Observant Minorites at Portoferraio on the Island of Elba, where it arrived transported by ship down the river Arno to the sea. At the far left, above, the bearded old man in the background is a self-portrait of the artist. The work survived in a deplorable state of conservation, having passed through numerous damaging events, starting with a devastating fire that broke out in the church, but a recent difficult, lengthy restoration (2003) has revealed again its significant artistic merit.

ALESSANDRO ALLORI
Annunciation

1578-1579
Oil on wood
445×285
Inv. 1890 no. 8662§

This panel, restored in 2003, was commissioned by Sister Laura de' Pazzi for the convent of Montedomini, in whose church it was situated when the holy institution was suppressed and its furnishings confiscated by the State. The severe and contained composition, suitable for a convent in a time of Counterreform, is softened by the charming still-life of the basket with clothes and the delicate flowers scattered on the floor.

Nineteenth Century Room

The large Nineteenth Century Room was conceived and realised in order to provide the collection of plaster casts by Lorenzo Bartolini with a stable and definitive location. However the intention was also to offer the visitor tangible evidence of the 19th century academic origins of this Gallery, today mainly known for Michelangelo's David.

Lorenzo Bartolini, *Demidoff Monument*

LORENZO BARTOLINI
Demidoff Monument
(whole on facing page
and details)

Post 1828
Plaster
Sculptures Inv. nos.
1174-1177, 1209, 1221

The commemorative
monument to Count
Nikolaj Demidoff was
commissioned by his
sons Paul and Anatolij
in 1828, on the death of
their father.
Due however to various
disruptions in the work,
several times interrupt-
ed and restarted when
the difficulties were over-
come, it was only placed
where it stands today (in
Piazza Demidoff, oppo-
site Lungarno Serristo-
ri) in 1871.
The work was finished
by Romanelli, a pupil of
Bartolini who took over
his workshop. It was a
grand and complex pro-
ject, consisting of ma-
ny statues, some larger
than life, with compli-
cated allegorical mean-
ing. The plaster model
of the central group, de-
picting the Count with
his son Anatolij, has been
lost.

61

LUIGI MUSSINI
Sacred Music
(whole and detail)

1841

Oil on canvas
150×104
Inv. Acc. no. 292/Cat. Gen.1

This is one of those paintings which testify to the original link between the Accademia Gallery and the Scuola dell'Accademia di Belle Arti (Academy of Fine Arts School). Mussini painted it in Rome in 1841 as a trial for his academic pension, and that same year it was exhibited in Florence in the Prizewinners' Gallery of the Accademia, where it remained for years. The subject of the painting is an angelic young man with wings who is gazing heavenward, his lips parted in a liturgical chant. The work is a manifest and illustrious example of Purism in Tuscany, and of how Luigi Mussini participated in the experience of the 'Nazarene' painters who drew inspiration from the great examples of 15th and early 16th century art. Mussini had also had the occasion to learn stylistic rigor in drawing directly from Ingres, during the time when this great artist was living in Florence in the 1820s.

Fourteenth Century Room

The Florentine Gothic painting route starts in these rooms, which house many gold-leaf background panels in an absolutely unique collection of its kind. Displayed in the central room are works by artists predating Giotto or his contemporaries, like Grifo di Tancredi and Pacino di Buonaguida; in the right-hand room are Giotto's direct followers, Taddeo Gaddi, Bernardo Daddi, Jacopo del Casentino in adition to a fresco by Giotto himself; in the left-hand room are the Orcagnas, Giovanni da Milano and Giottino.

**Master
of Santa Cecilia**
Enthroned Madonna

c. 1310-1320
Tempera on wood
185×97
Inv. 1890 no. 5917

This is a work of fundamental importance for the history of 14th century Florentine painting. It is attributed to an anonymous contemporary and collaborator of Giotto, whose hand is recognisable also in some parts of the frescoes with *Scenes from the Life of Saint Francis* in the upper basilica of San Francesco in Assisi.

PACINO
DI BUONAGUIDA
Tree of Life
(whole and details
on the right)

c.1305-1310

Tempera on wood
248×151
Inv. 1890 no. 8459

With its vivid colours and sophisticated drawing (Pacino was also a famous illuminator), this painting mainly illustrates the content of Saint Bonaventure's *Lignum Vitae*, although there are also many scenes and scrolls alluding to biblical texts. In its entirety it appears as a large doctrinal page for meditation as well as an image to be admired. The subject of the illustration is the genealogy of Christ, who is shown nailed to the tree-shaped cross with its roots on a rocky mountain, symbolising Mt. Calvary.

**MASTER
OF THE MAGDALENE**
*Mary Magdalene
and Scenes
from her Life*

c. 1280-1285

Tempera on wood
164×76
Inv. 1890 no. 8466

This panel clearly exemplifies Florentine painting before Giotto, within whose circle this anonymous painter can be placed.

Giotto set up one of the most productive workshops in Florence between 1265 and 1290, and this painter also shows evidence of attention to the innovations introduced by Cimabue.

In this sense, the small side scenes, which offer a direct and lively narrative of moments from the saint's life, are more attractive than the solemn central figure. A conspicuous example are the naturalistic landscape elements in the background of the *Noli me tangere* (depicted in the second scene on the left).

GIOTTO
AND ASSISTANTS
Shepherd
with his flocks

1315-1325

Detached fresco
250×135
From the church of Badia
in Florence

This fragment of a detached fresco comes from the ancient high chapel of the church of Badia in Florence which, according to Ghiberti and other sources earlier than Giorgio Vasari, was frescoed by Giotto, who also painted the polyptych over the high altar, now in the Uffizi Gallery. In the past this and a few other surviving pictorial fragments were not unanimously accepted by critics as authentic works by Giotto, but in recent years the pictorial quality of this shepherd's head – originally belonging in all probability to the scene of Joachim among the shepherds – has been noted by the greatest scholars of Giotto's art. More than one expert has observed at most a certain stylistic diversity between the Uffizi polyptych, a key work in the development of Giotto's style around the year 1300, and this fragment, whose freshness and luminosity point to a substantially later dating, perhaps during the span of time between the painting of the frescoes in the Peruzzi chapel (c. 1310-1315) and those in the Bardi chapel (c. 1325-1330) in the Florentine basilica of Santa Croce.

JACOPO DEL CASENTINO
Saint Bartholomew

c.1340

Tempera on wood
266×122
Inv. 1890 no. 440

This panel was commissioned straight after 1339 by the Grocers' Guild, who at that very time had erected their shrine on one of the pillars of the church of Orsanmichele and dedicated it to their patron, Saint Bartholomew. The pillars of the whole church of Orsanmichele were decorated during the 14th century with images of the patron saints of the various Guilds: this is because it was the delegated area for trade and its upper floor was actually used as a granary while the market was held in the loggia on the ground floor.

The saint's face has been considerably damaged by cleaning with soda, presumably in the last century but fortunately the inexpert restorer must have realised the harm he was doing and refrained from continuing, as the rest of the panel is well-preserved.

BERNARDO DADDI
*Saint Bartholomew
and Saint Lawrence*

c. 1340

Tempera on wood
104×39.5 (each panel)
Inv. 1890 nos. 8706 and 8707

These two saints were part of a polyptych made for the chapel of Saint Bartholomew and Saint Lawrence in the church of the Carmine in Florence; at the polyptych's centre was a *Madonna with Child* and at the sides two or perhaps four *Saints*. The polyp-tych also probably had a predella.

These paintings reach-ed us in an exception-ally integral state of pre-servation and allow us to fully appreciate the quality of Bernardo Daddi's work in around 1340, at the peak of his career.

BERNARDO DADDI
Crucifix

c. 1348
Tempera on wood
350×275
Inv. 1890 no. 442

This large, shaped crucifix possibly comes from the church of San Donato in Polverosa and was presumably placed above the high altar, hanging from the ceiling. In medieval churches this type of image was often placed on top of the iconostasis, i.e. the dividing wall between the presbytery and the choir, as is clearly shown in the Greccio nativity scene painted by Giotto in the basilica of San Francesco in Assisi.

70

TADDEO GADDI
*Stories from
the Life of Christ
and of Saint Francis*
(*Crucifixion,
Adoration of the Magi,
Stigmata of Saint Francis,
Saint Francis upholds
the Church*)

c. 1333

Tempera on wood
41×29/36 (panels),
72×158 (lunettes)
Inv. 1890 nos. 8581-8603

These panels came from the sacristy of the basilica of Santa Croce where they decorated wooden furniture, perhaps a reliquary cupboard.
The single episodes from the life of Saint Francis are illustrated in a parallel with the life of Christ: for example, the episode with the imposition of the stigmata corresponds to the *Crucifixion*. Taddeo Gaddi, Giotto's most direct pupil, was the first to include his master's innovations: note the solid volumetric disposition of the figures and the well-constructed architectural perspective, which indicate a *modus operandi* very far removed from the transcendent and ethereal world of Byzantine painting.

ANDREA ORCAGNA
Pentecost
(whole and detail)

c. 1365

Tempera on wood
195×287
Deposits Inv. no. 165

This triptych reveals the characteristics of Andrea Orcagna's painting style in the last phase of his life; with its square spaces, the rigid frontal arrangement of the figures and the limited chromatic range, it must have fitted harmoniously in the Romanesque church of the Santi Apostoli in Florence, where it came from. In the second half of the 18th century it was transferred to the church of Badia, from where it was passed to the Accademia Gallery in 1939. It is likely that Andrea's younger brother Jacopo assisted in the painting work, and his hand can be seen in areas of softer, more blended application of colour in some of the apostles, and hints of softness in the volumetric construction.

NARDO DI CIONE
The Trinity

1365
Tempera on wood
300×210
Inv. 1890 no. 8464

This impressive polyptych was commissioned by Giovanni Ghiberti for his chapel in the Chapter of Santa Maria degli Angeli. It was removed from there in about 1750 and taken to the Della Stufa chapel, dedicated to Saint Andrew, and on this occasion Saint John was repainted to resemble Saint Andrew. Today the triptych has resumed its original appearance.

JACOPO DI CIONE
*Stories from the
Childhood of Christ*

c.1370

Tempera on wood
141×101
Inv. 1890 no. 5887

This panel was in the past attributed to an anonymous master, known as the Maestro dell'Infanzia di Cristo [Master of Christ's Childhood], because of the scenes depicted here, but has now been included in the early works of Jacopo di Cione, brother of Andrea Orcagna and quite close in his lively narrative style to Niccolò di Tommaso.

**JACOPO DI CIONE
AND ASSISTANTS**
*Coronation
of the Virgin*

c. 1370

Tempera on wood
350×190
Inv. 1890 no. 456

This large panel was commissioned by the officials of the Mint, where the gold coin of Florence was struck (the florin). Gold, in fact, plays an important role in this luminous composition in which the throne disappears behind decorated tapestry drapery with naturalistic and geometric elements, sophisticated enough to be worthy of the most flamboyant Gothicism.

GIOVANNI DA MILANO
Christ in Pietà
1365

Tempera on wood; 122×58
Inv. 1890 no. 8467

This small devotional panel represents one of the greatest achievements of 14th century painting in Florence after the death of Giotto.

It was painted for the church of San Girolamo alla Costa, dated and signed, and at the bottom bears the coats of arms of the Strozzi and Rinieri families who obviously commissioned it. Giovanni da Milano's painting, with its intense sensitivity to colour and

moving sentimentality offers an alternative to the severe style of Orcagna, which had dominated the gloomy period following the Great Plague of 1348. With Giovanni's work, Florence opened up to the new insistence of the International Gothic trend.

ANDREA DI BONAIUTO
Saint Agnes
and Saint Domitilla

c. 1365-1370

Tempera on wood
66×28
Inv. 1890 no. 3145

Andrea di Bonaiuto (also known as Andrea da Firenze), a Florentine painter who trained in the studio of Nardo di Cione, brother of Andrea Orcagna, is famous above all for having frescoed the Spagnuoli Chapel in the Santa Maria Novella monastery. This small diptych is stylistically and therefore chronologically close to that work and demonstrates the painter's knowledge and assimilation of the work of Giovanni da Milano, who was present and working in Florence in those very years.

The two female figures shown here particularly stand out for the courtly sophistication of their costly clothes and the intense use of chiaroscuro.

MATTEO DI PACINO
*Vision of
Saint Bernard*

(whole and detail)

c. 1365
Tempera on wood
173×199
Inv. 1890 no. 8463

The panel, attributed in the past to an anonymous Master of the Rinuccini Chapel, is now recognized as the work of Matteo di Pacino, a painter trained in the Orcagna shop and thus possessing a style marked by a strong sense of volumetric disposition and monumentality, who worked with Giovanni da Milano on the fresco decorations of the Rinuccini Chapel in Santa Croce, completing them when da Milano left Florence. Due to his contact with Giovanni da Milano, the painter's chromatic range is warmer and brighter than that of Orcagna's closest followers.

First Floor Rooms (Late Gothic Art)

These recently restored and rearranged rooms bring together the varied and exhaustive range of late Gothic Florentine painting.
These include portable altarpieces and grand polyptychs, as well as a collection of twelve works by Lorenzo Monaco, an incomparably beautiful group of exceptional rarity, through which we can become familiar with the work of this great Gothic painter in all the phases of his artistic career.

LATE FOURTEENTH CENTURY ROOM 1

DON SILVESTRO DE' GHERARDUCCI
Madonna of Humility

c.1370-1375
Tempera on wood
164×89
Inv. 1890 no. 3161

Silvestro de' Gherarducci entered the monastery of Santa Maria degli Angioli in 1348 aged nine. He worked with Lorenzo Monaco as a painter and illuminator, never losing the characteristic rich and colourful decorative elements which denote his Sienese origins. The *Virgin of Humility*, which depicts the Virgin Mary sitting on the ground on a cushion, is a subject particularly dear to late Gothic tastes.

GIOVANNI DEL BIONDO
Annunciation
(whole and detail)

c. 1380-1385

Tempera on wood
406×377
Inv. 1890 no. 8606

This large and complex polyptych was situated on the altar of the Cavalcanti chapel in Santa Maria Novella. It came to us in excellent condition, complete with almost all its accessories, and constitutes an example of the high technical quality of the work of 14th century Florentine workshops.

MARIOTTO DI NARDO
Madonna and Child
Enthroned with Saints

c. 1390-1395

Tempera on wood
165×242 (central part),
42×267 (predella)
Inv. 1890 nos. 8612,
3260, 3258, 3259

This polyptych records the mature phase of Mariotto di Nardo, an active artist in Florence between the 14th and 15th centuries, also for important commissions. His success was probably due to the Orcagnesque elements in his style, whose excessive hardness was diluted with warmer colouring and more charming decorative elements. This work has reached us complete with all its elements (predella and cuspidate panels). It gives some idea of how ornate the altars of the most important Medieval churches must have been.

NICCOLÒ
DI PIETRO GERINI
*Christ as the Man
of Sorrows, with the
Symbols of the Passion*
(on the left)

c. 1404-1408
Tempera on wood
351×158
Inv. 1890 nos. 5048, 5066, 5067

This panel is a typical example of the work of the Orcagna-trained painter Niccolò di Pietro Gerini and comes from the Disciplinary Company of the Pellegrino in Santa Maria Novella. The brethren of the company are depicted on the cusp kneeling in the foreground before Christ dressed as a pilgrim, and on the predella in the act of burying one of the members of their Company. All the brethren wear white cloaks and their heads are covered by hoods, in order not to be recognised while carrying out works of charity.

At the centre Christ rises from the tomb, showing the wounds in his hands and side, before the cross, on which are hung the symbols of the Passion: nails, whips, the spear and the sponge.

SPINELLO ARETINO
Saint Stephen

c. 1400-1405
Tempera on wood
92×33
Inv. 1890 no. 6287

The saint is depicted holding in his right hand the banner of the Wool Guild, which was quite a powerful corporation in Florence and the same motif is repeated on the sides of the predella. This little tabernacle demonstrates the preciosity of Spinello's later style, and to a greater extent, the small Crucifixion in the cusp panel, where the drapery of the crouching figures flows with inimitable elegance.

**ROSSELLO
DI JACOPO FRANCHI**

*Coronation
of the Virgin*

(whole and detail)

1422

Tempera on wood
344×300
Inv. 1890 no. 8460

This grand and highly decorated polyptych is the work of Rossello di Jacopo Franchi, an artist who trained in the late Gothic period and continued to paint his sweet and rather mannered figures until the end of his life (1456), long after the advent in Florence of Masaccio and the rise of the early Renaissance.

LORENZO MONACO
*The Prayer
in the Garden*

c. 1395

Tempera on wood
222×109
Inv. 1890 no. 438

This is one of the oldest panels by Lorenzo Monaco and was painted for the Florentine monastery of Santa Maria degli Angioli, where the artist lived. His deep knowledge of Giotto's painting, who must have been directly known to him, is evident from the style, learned in the Orcagna studio. However, at the same time the fluid and extended flowing of the drapery places his work within the modern taste for International Gothicism.

85

LORENZO MONACO
Enthroned Madonna with Saints

1410

Tempera on wood
274×259
Inv. 1890 no. 468

This polyptych formerly decorated the church of San Bartolomeo in Montoliveto near Florence and confirms Lorenzo Monaco's ability with chromatic and decorative effects, even in works of larger dimensions. Having now fully mastered his expressive medium, the great master emphasises here the outlines of the figures with impeccable fluidity and harmony while the chromatic range seems infused with the purest light. It must be remembered that Lorenzo Monaco was also an illuminator and his pen decorated with gold and bright colours many of the manuscripts made in the monastery of Santa Maria degli Angioli, where he lived as a Camaldolensian monk.

LORENZO MONACO
Annunciation
(whole and detail)

c. 1418
Tempera on wood
210×229
Inv. 1890 no. 8458

Painted for the Florentine Badia, this *Annunciation* represents the peak of Lorenzo Monaco's work; in the period in which Masaccio, who began the artistic Renaissance, was beginning to work, the medieval world is brought to life with brilliant success in this work.

**MASTER
OF THE STRAUS
MADONNA**
Annunciation
(whole and detail)

c. 1395-1405
190×200
Inv. 1890 no. 3146

This work came from the leper Hospital of Sant'Eusebio al Prato and is attributed to a painter who was active between the end of the 14th century and the beginning of the 15th century.

His identity is not known and he is usually known as the Master of the Straus Madonna from a *Madonna with Child* formerly in the Straus collection. This is a painter of a very high standard, gifted with fine sensitivity to colour and who also pays attention to the volumetric structure of bodies and the perspective depth of the space.

GHERARDO STARNINA
Enthroned Madonna
and Child with
St. John the Baptist,
St. Nicholas and Angels

c. 1407-1410
Tempera on wood
96×51
Inv. 1890 no. 441

Gherardo Starnina, a Florentine painter who also worked in Spain where he came into contact with the most advanced trends of International Gothicism, today tends to be identified by critics as the so-called Master of Bam-

bin Vispo [Lively Child], an outstanding figure in early 15th century painting in Florence. He was noted for his linear finesse and the decorative nature of his elegant forms, and is almost a profane *alter ego* of Lorenzo Monaco.

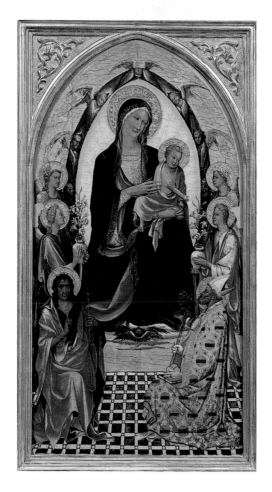

GIOVANNI TOSCANI
*The Incredulity
of Saint Thomas*

c. 1420
Tempera on wood
240×112
Inv. 1890 no. 457

Giovanni Toscani was for a long time known as the Master of the Griggs Crucifixion, before his identity was discovered in 1966. The subject matter of this panel is commented on the dado at the bottom with the words 'Touch that which is real like me and you will believe in justice combined in three people, which always exalts those who act justly'. The sentence refers to a place where justice was administered, perhaps the Court of Mercatanzia, around which he worked in 1419-1420; this date is in keeping with the Gothic characteristics of the work.

BICCI DI LORENZO
Saint Lawrence

c. 1428

Tempera on wood
236×84
Inv. 1890 no. 471

This panel comes from the laical company devoted to Saint Peter at the church of San Pietro a Monticelli.

The saint Lawrence is shown standing on the symbol of his martyrdom, the grille, while in his left hand he holds the palm and in the right a red banner with a gold star, perhaps the insignia of the Company who commissioned the work. In the predella, in the right-hand scene, Saint Lawrence is depicted freeing souls from Purgatory, according to the legend which claims that as he died on Good Friday, he was permitted every Friday to repeat Christ's descent to the underworld. The scene on the left shows the martyrdom inflicted on him by his persecutors.

Bicci di Lorenzo painted this work in collaboration with Stefano d'Antonio with whom he "kept company" (or as we would say today "was in partnership") from 1426 to 1434.

THE COLLECTION OF ICONS

The collection of icons is displayed along the stairs, on the landings and in display cases. MAny of them were made in Russia and come from the Guardarobe of the Grand Dukes of Lorraine. The quality of these pieces is rather discontinuous and only rarely of exceptional calibre; therefore it might be said that the group as a whole is more significant for research and knowledge of the Lorraine passion for collecting rather than for the history of Russian art.

ANDREA RITZOS DA CANDIA
Madonna of the Passion (Madonna and Child, Angels and the Instruments of the Passion)

15th century
Mixed technique on wood
70×54
Inv. 1890 no. 3886

The icon is signed by the renowned painter

from Crete active in the 15th century in Candia. The painting comes from the Franciscan monastery of San Girolamo at Fiesole (Florence).

RUSSIAN SCHOOL
*Saint Catherine
of Alexandria*

Late 17th century
Tempera on wood
32×27
Inv. 1890 no. 5979

Saint Catherine is portrayed with her usual attributes, i.e. the palm of martyrdom in her right hand and the hooked wheel on which she was tortured in her left.

The icon was made in the workshops of the Armoury Palace in Moscow. Punching on the silver-gilt frame indicates the date as 1693-1694.

INDEX